Disney
Winnie the Pooh

"Good morning, Piglet," said Winnie the Pooh.
"Good morning, Pooh," replied Piglet.
Pooh and Piglet were best friends. They were happy together in the Hundred-Acre Wood.

"Pooh, I've made us a haycorn pie," said Piglet.
"Mmmm," said Pooh. "Shall we put some honey on it?"
The two friends sat down to eat.

After he had finished every drop of honey, Pooh stood up.

"I'm very tired," he said. "I'd like to have a nap now."

"Good idea, Pooh," replied Piglet. "But how about going for a walk first?"

"Alright then, Piglet. Off we go," said Pooh, stretching and yawning.

Pooh and Piglet had an adventure every time they went for a walk.

In the autumn, Pooh and Piglet played in the leaves.

In the winter, they made snow angels.

In the spring, they enjoyed watching the Hundred-Acre Wood turn green again.

In the summer, they picked pretty flowers.

Sometimes, Pooh and Piglet would go and visit their other friends. They often went to eat at Rabbit's house.

They listened to Owl telling stories.

They helped Kanga with her knitting.

And they flew kites with Christopher Robin.
Wherever Pooh went, Piglet went too.

Today, as they set off for their walk, a bee flew by. Pooh followed the bee to find some honey.

At the same time, a beautiful butterfly flew past in the other direction.

Piglet ran after the butterfly.

Piglet looked through his binoculars. He watched the colourful butterfly with the pretty wings flying from flower to flower.

"Would you like to see the butterfly through my binoculars, Pooh?" Piglet asked without looking behind him. He thought Pooh was there. "What a lovely creature!"

Piglet turned to the tree where Pooh usually liked to sleep. But Pooh wasn't there. He was nowhere to be seen!
"Oh, dear!" said Piglet, surprised. "Where are you, Pooh?"

"Where in the world has Pooh gone without me?" said Piglet to himself.

He rushed off to find him, even though he didn't know where to start looking.

Meanwhile, Pooh was busy with the bee, or rather a swarm of bees!

But before long, he started to worry about Piglet too.

Pooh hurried off to find his friend.

At last, Pooh and Piglet found each other on the path through the Hundred-Acre Wood.

"There you are, Pooh!" cried Piglet. "Where have you been?"

"I'm not sure," replied Pooh, "but I'm so glad to see you again, Piglet!"

"We'll have to remember to say goodbye next time," said Piglet, smiling.

"You're right!" replied Pooh.

The two friends were very glad to see each other again.
"Together or apart, we're best friends," said Piglet.
"Yes, we are," agreed Pooh.
"What would you like to do tomorrow?" asked Piglet.
"Let's meet to have breakfast," said Pooh.
"Great idea!" said Piglet. "And then we can go for a walk."
"Wonderful!" said Pooh.